Discovery Kids

CUTEST DOGS OF ALL TIME

by Mari Bolte

PEBBLE
a capstone imprint

Published by Pebble, an imprint of Capstone
1710 Roe Crest Drive, North Mankato, Minnesota 56003
capstonepub.com

Library of Congress Cataloging-in-Publication Data is available on the Library of Congress website.

ISBN: 9798875256585 (hardcover)
ISBN: 9798875256530 (paperback)
ISBN: 9798875256547 (ebook PDF)

Summary: Sixteen dog breeds face off in a challenge to find out which pup is the C.O.A.T.—Cutest of All Time. Each featured dog receives a score of one to five in three categories for an overall cute factor score.

Editorial Credits
Editor: Erika L. Shores; Designer: Dina Her; Media Researcher: Rebekah Hubstenberger; Production Specialist: Tori Abraham

Image Credits
Getty Images: iStock/Aleksandra Pankina, 21 (dog), 22, iStock/cynoclub, back cover (left), 15; Shutterstock: Africa Studio, front cover (bottom middle), Anton Vierietin, 1 (right), 5, 14 (dog), Csanad Kiss, 18, E LLL, 3 (left), 13, Eric Isselee, front cover (bottom right and left), back cover (top right), 6, 8 (dog), 11, 19 (dog), Evgeniya89, front cover (doodle bow-tie), Giuseppe_R, front cover (doodle glasses), GPPets, 9 (dog), kichikimi (dog bowl, treats), 10, 13, KYRYCHENKO ANASTASIIA (doodle glasses), 1, 9, lesyau_art (stars and ribbon medal), throughout, Look_Studio (doodle birthday hat, heart flag, flowers, hearts, candy), front cover and throughout, LORA MARCHENKO, 14 (doodle accessories), MirasWonderland, 12 (dog), mydesign94, 12 (doodle scuba mask), Nadiinko (twinkle stars), front and back cover, 1, Nynke van Holten, 3 (right), Polina Tomtosova (doodle hearts, shapes, lines, shooting star), back cover and throughout, Rita_Kochmarjova, 4, Stokkete, 16, TrapezaStudio, 17, Viorel Sima, 1 (left), 7 (dog), 10, Voin_Sveta, 21 (crown), wasapohn (doodle hat), 1, 8, Zaie (dot background), cover and throughout

Printed in the United States 6724

CUTES FACE OFF

Dogs are cute. But which dog **breed** is the Cutest Of All Time (C.O.A.T.)?

We matched 16 perfect pups in a face-off of who's cuter. Each dog gets one to five stars in three categories. Read to find out each dog's total score. Then use the chart at the end to see which pup is the C.O.A.T.!

BASSET HOUND

What's that smelly smell? A basset hound's sense of smell is one of the best. It's not just a long nose that helps this hound smell. Long ears drag on the ground. They stir up smells for the nose to sniff.

Cutest Thing About Me:
Super saggy skin!

Fluffiness: ★★☆☆☆

Aww Factor: ★★★★★

Cuddle-ability: ★★★★★

Total Cute Factor: 12

Cutest Thing About Me:
Super fluffy double coat!

Fluffiness: ★★★★☆
Aww Factor: ★★☆☆☆
Cuddle-ability: ★★★★★

Total Cute Factor: 11

AUSTRALIAN SHEPHERD

Their name makes them sound like they live with kangaroos. But “Aussies” really come from California. They are **herding** dogs. That means they love telling other animals where to go.

CORGI

Corgis are long and low. They have short, little legs and long, heavy bodies. Corgis relax on their tummies. Then they stretch their back legs straight out. People call it splooting. So cute!

CAVALIER KING CHARLES SPANIEL

These royal pups were loved by King Charles II of England. He had a pack of spaniels that followed him everywhere. Today's Cavaliers are just as loyal. They love their job of being the perfect family pet.

Cutest Thing About Me:
Long ears covered in silky hair!

Fluffiness: ★☆☆☆☆

Aww Factor: ★★★★★

Cuddle-ability: ★★★★★

Total Cute Factor: 11

CHIHUAHUA

Chihuahuas are little. Adults weigh only 3 to 6 pounds (1.4 to 2.7 kilograms). They can fit easily in small purses and bags. Hello! One Chihuahua, just tagging along for the day!

Cutest Thing About Me:
Likes to play dress-up!

Fluffiness: ★☆☆☆☆

Aww Factor: ★★★★★

Cuddle-ability: ★★★★☆

Total Cute Factor: 10

HUSKY

It's a snow day, and no one is happier than a husky. Huskies have thick, **double coats** to keep them warm. Their padded paws are also furry. Huskies like to dig snow forts. Fun now, nap later!

Cutest Thing About Me:
Pointy fox ears!

Fluffiness: ★★★★★
Aww Factor: ★★★★★
Cuddle-ability: ★★☆☆☆

Total Cute Factor: 12

GREYHOUND

Greyhounds have been around since ancient Egypt, 5,000 years ago. They are the fastest dog breed. They used to hunt speedy animals, such as gazelles. Today, they just hunt their favorite toys.

Cutest Thing About Me:
Extra-long neck and nose!

Fluffiness: ★☆☆☆☆

Aww Factor: ★★★☆☆

Cuddle-ability: ★★★★☆

Total Cute Factor: 8

Cutest Thing About Me:
Fluffy double coat!

Fluffiness: ★★★★★
Aww Factor: ★★★★★
Cuddle-ability: ★★★★☆

Total Cute Factor: 14

POMERANIAN

Pomeranians are related to dogs that pull sleds in the snow. But Poms are too small to help out. They weigh 7 pounds (3 kg) or less. They are the perfect breed to help people as **therapy** dogs. Who's a good dog?

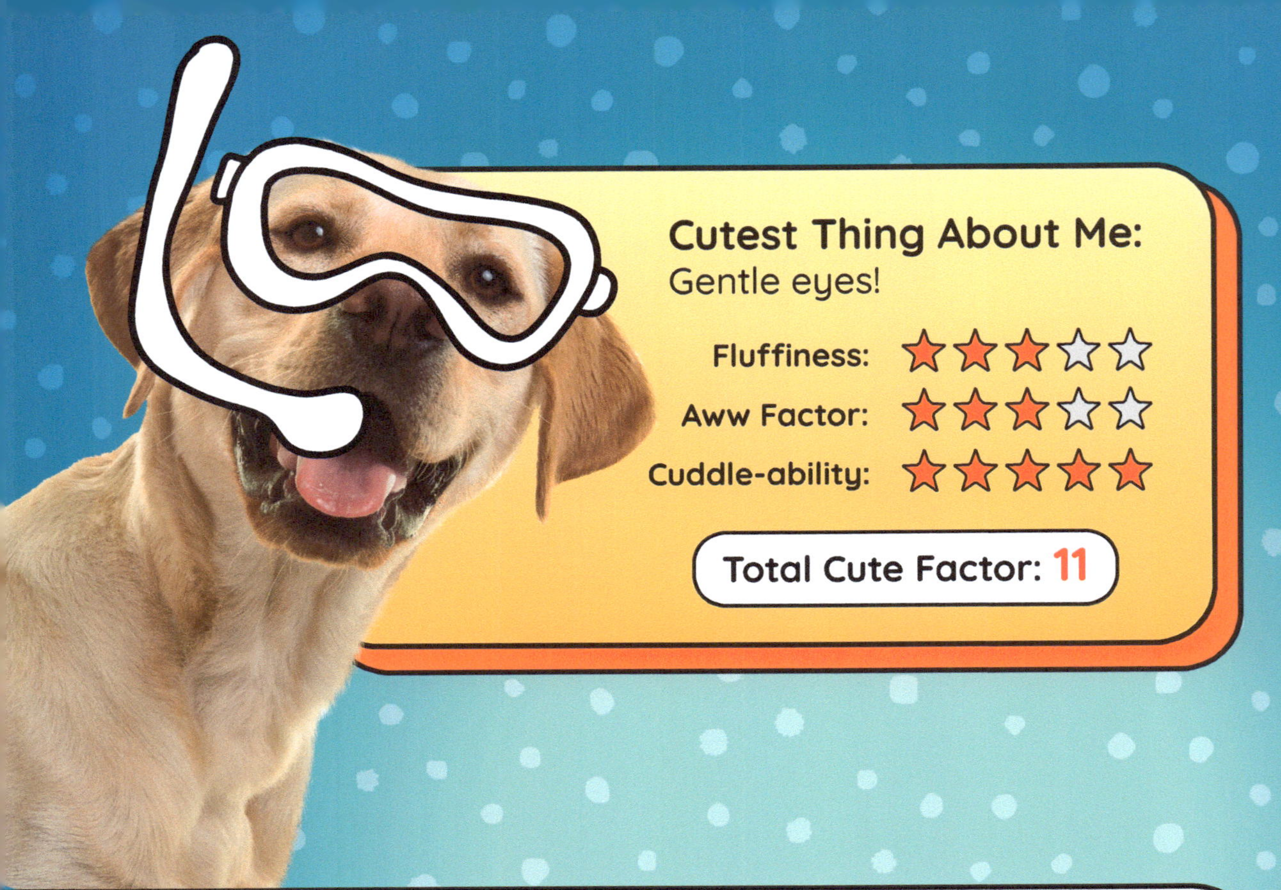

LABRADOR RETRIEVER

Labs are friendly and playful. They like to play fetch. And they love to go swimming. They will find the nearest pond, pool, or puddle and hop right in. Splash!

ST. BERNARD

Do you need help? Call a St. Bernard! These giant dogs were bred to rescue people in snowy mountains. Today, some are trained to help in **search-and-rescue** missions. They also are gentle and calm therapy dogs. Who wouldn't want to hug a St. Bernard?

Cutest Thing About Me:
Like a big teddy bear!

Fluffiness: ★★★★★
Aww Factor: ★★★★☆
Cuddle-ability: ★★★★★

Total Cute Factor: 14

PUG

Look at all those wrinkles! Pugs have smooshy faces. Those short noses mean sleeping pugs are full of snores. Sometimes they even snort themselves awake.

Cutest Thing About Me:
Curlicue tail!

Fluffiness: ★☆☆☆☆

Aww Factor: ★★★★☆

Cuddle-ability: ★★★★☆

Total Cute Factor: 9

CHOW CHOW

Help! A lion has escaped from the zoo! Oh, that's just a chow chow. This breed's thick coat looks like a lion's **mane.** Does a lion have a blue tongue? No, but a chow chow does!

Cutest Thing About Me:
A nose for trouble!

Fluffiness: ★☆☆☆☆
Aww Factor: ★★★★★
Cuddle-ability: ★★★★★

Total Cute Factor: 11

DACHSHUND

Some people call Dachshunds wiener dogs or sausage dogs. And if you don’t watch out, these little dogs will steal snacks right out of your hand. Dachshunds are determined. If they want something, they will do anything to get it.

BORZOI

Borzois are fast and beautiful. They have long, silky coats and a body built for speed. Watch out, squirrels. A borzoi is on the loose.

Cutest Thing About Me:
Long, pointy nose!

Fluffiness: ★☆☆☆☆

Aww Factor: ★★★★☆

Cuddle-ability: ★★★★☆

Total Cute Factor: 9

GREAT DANE

Is that a mini horse? No, it's a great big dog! Great Danes can weigh 175 pounds (79 kilograms). But don't even think about riding one of these gentle giants. Try giving them cuddles instead.

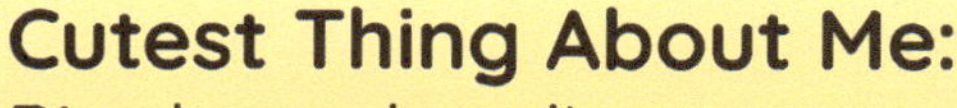

Cutest Thing About Me:
Big dopey head!

Fluffiness: ★☆☆☆☆

Aww Factor: ★★★★★

Cuddle-ability: ★★★★★

Total Cute Factor: 11

OLD ENGLISH SHEEPDOG

Baa or bark? Old English sheepdogs were bred to guard sheep. The dogs' fluffy coats help them blend in with the herd. Patient sheepdogs are always on the lookout for danger.

Cutest Thing About Me:
Floofy face!

Fluffiness:	★★★★★
Aww Factor:	★★★★☆
Cuddle-ability:	★★★★★

Total Cute Factor: 14

CUTE FACTOR FACE OFF

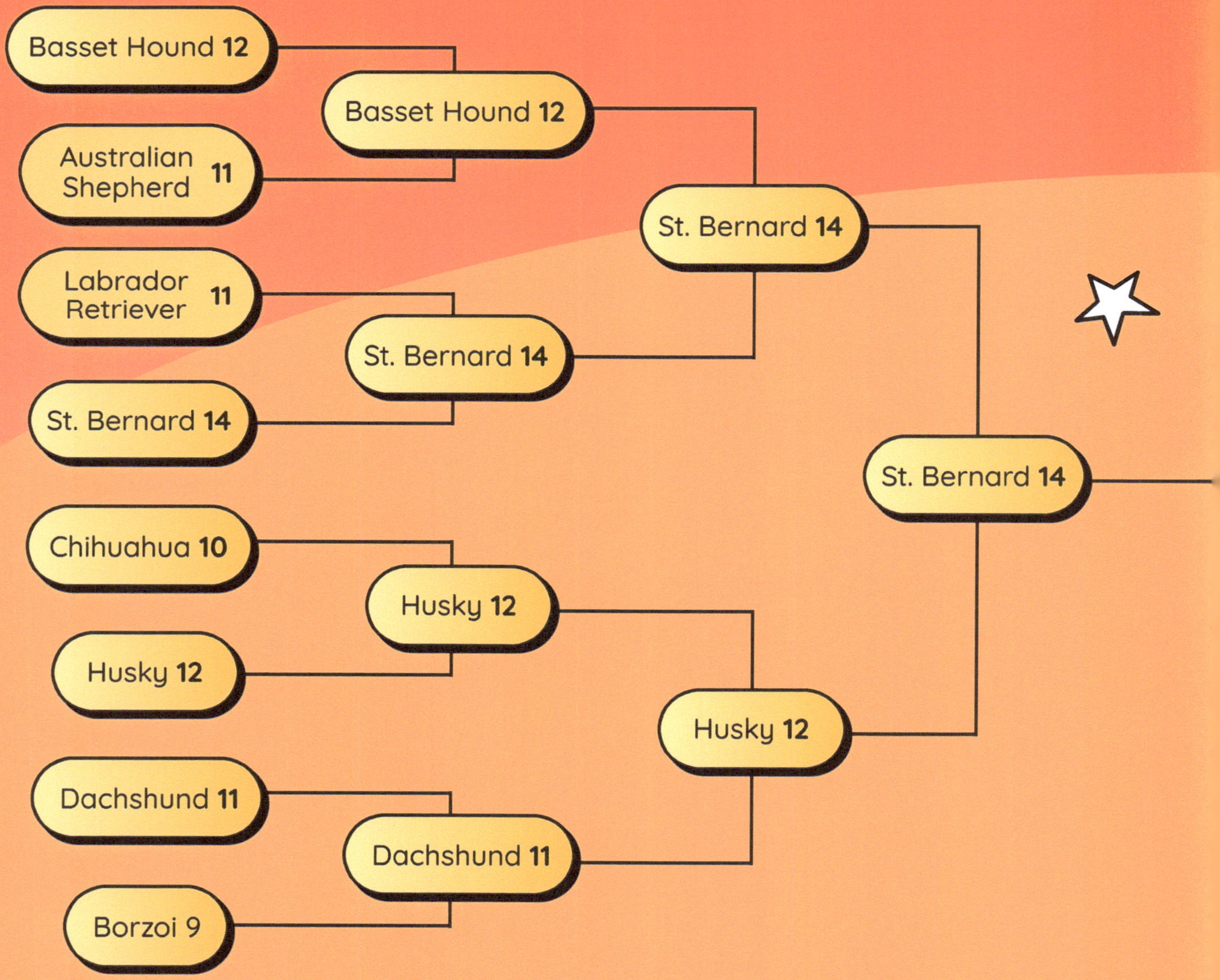

Basset Hound **12**

Australian Shepherd **11**

Labrador Retriever **11**

St. Bernard **14**

Chihuahua **10**

Husky **12**

Dachshund **11**

Borzoi 9

Basset Hound **12**

St. Bernard **14**

Husky **12**

Dachshund **11**

St. Bernard **14**

Husky **12**

St. Bernard **14**

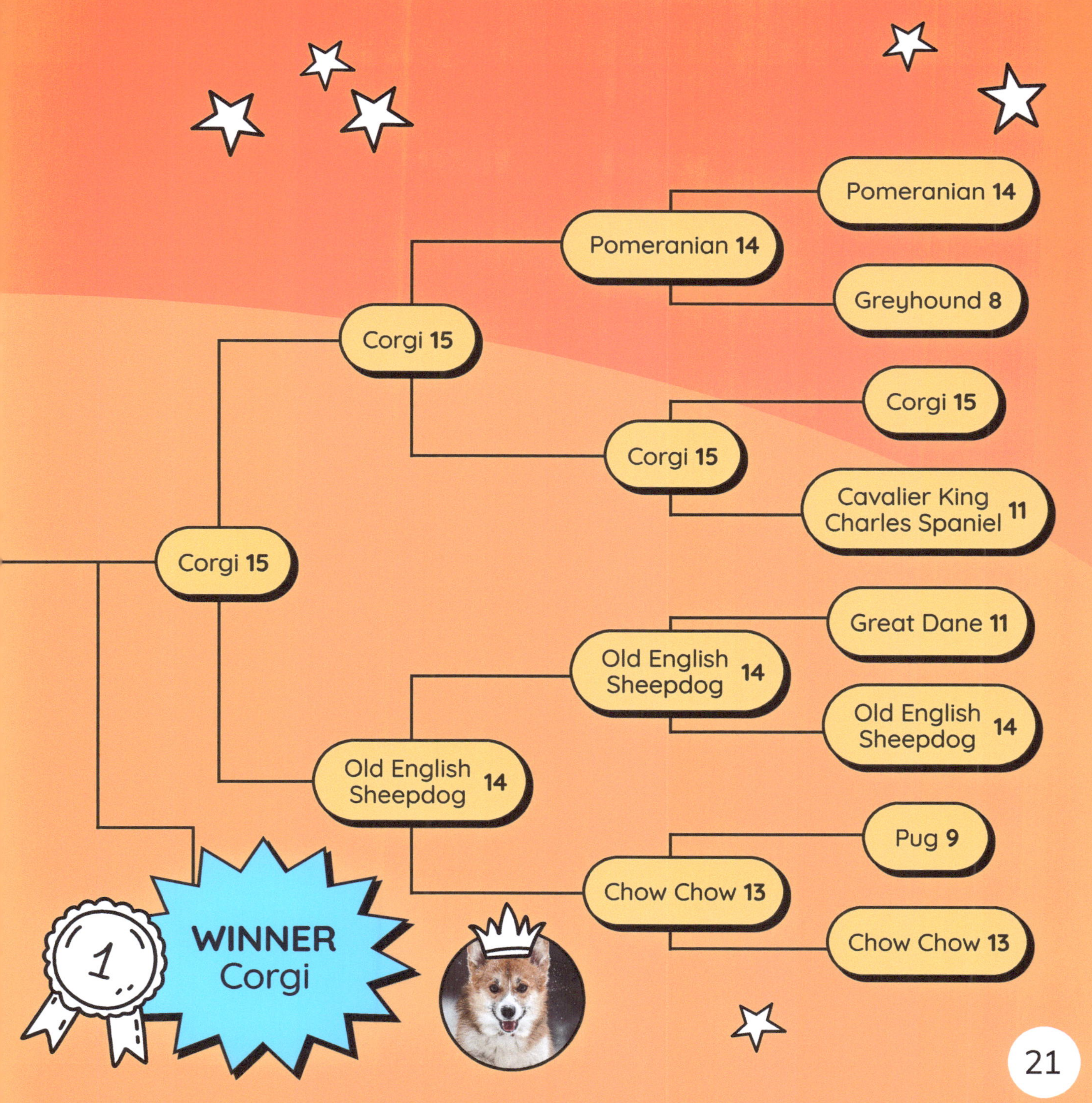
Pomeranian 14
Pomeranian 14
Greyhound 8
Corgi 15
Corgi 15
Corgi 15
Cavalier King Charles Spaniel 11
Corgi 15
Great Dane 11
Old English Sheepdog 14
Old English Sheepdog 14
Old English Sheepdog 14
Pug 9
Chow Chow 13
Chow Chow 13
1
WINNER
Corgi

THE C.O.A.T.

Which pup wagged its way to the top? Corgis made a mad dash on four little legs and won the race! They are officially the Cutest Of All Time!

Do you agree? Go back and give each dog your own score. Grab some paper and make a new chart. Maybe a different pup will be your winner.

GLOSSARY

breed (BREED)—a group of animals within a species that share the same features, such as color or markings

double coat (DUH-buhl KOHT)—a coat that is thick and soft close to the skin and covered with lighter, silky fur on the top

herding (HER-ding)—a type of dog trained to control the movement of other animals

mane (MAYN)—long, thick hair that grows on the head and neck of some animals like lions and horses

search-and-rescue (SURCH-AND-res-CUE)—searching for and aiding people who are in danger or need help

therapy (THER-uh-pee)—a treatment for an illness, an injury, or a disability

INDEX

Australian shepherds, 5

basset hounds, 4

Borzois, 17

Cavalier King Charles spaniels, 7

Chihuahuas, 8

chow chows, 15

Corgis, 6, 22

Dachshunds, 16

Great Danes, 18

greyhounds, 10

huskies, 9

Labrador retrievers, 12

Old English sheepdogs, 19

Pomeranians, 11

pugs, 14

St. Bernards, 13

ABOUT THE AUTHOR

Mari Bolte is the author and editor of hundreds of children's books. Every book is her favorite book as long as the readers learned something and enjoyed themselves!